The Business Of Family Caregiving

Introduction

In recent decades, global demographics have shifted dramatically, leading to a significant increase in the aging population.

According to the United Nations, by 2050, the number of people aged 65 and older is expected to more than double, reaching over 1.5 billion.

This demographic shift is particularly pronounced in developed countries, where advancements in healthcare and living conditions have extended life expectancy.

However, this rise in the elderly population has also brought about numerous challenges, particularly in the realm of elder care.

As people live longer, they are more likely to experience chronic health conditions such as heart disease, diabetes, and dementia.

These conditions often require ongoing care, which places a considerable burden on healthcare systems and families.

The traditional model of elder care, which heavily relied on nursing homes and assisted living facilities, is becoming increasingly unsustainable.

The costs associated with institutional care are rising, and many families are seeking alternative solutions that allow them to care for their loved ones at home.

Rising Need for Elder Care

The demand for elder care is surging as the population ages. In the United States alone, the number of people requiring long-term care services is projected to grow from 12 million in 2020 to over 27 million by 2050.

Similar trends are being observed in Europe, Japan, and other regions with aging populations.

This increase in demand has put immense pressure on healthcare systems, leading to a shortage of professional caregivers and a rise in the cost of care.

Moreover, the COVID-19 pandemic has highlighted the vulnerabilities of institutional elder care settings, where outbreaks have led to high mortality rates among residents.

As a result, more families are reconsidering the benefits of home care, where they can provide personalized attention and ensure the safety of their elderly relatives.

This shift toward family caregiving is part of a broader trend that is reshaping the landscape of elder care globally.

Section 1: The Shift Toward Family Care

The care of elderly family members has historically been a family responsibility across many cultures.

In agrarian societies, older adults were often cared for by their children or extended family members within multigenerational households.

This arrangement provided a sense of security and continuity, allowing elders to remain integrated within their communities while receiving the support they needed.

In many Asian, African, and Middle Eastern cultures, filial piety—respect and care for one's parents and ancestors—has been a core value, deeply influencing family structures and caregiving practices.

In contrast, the Western world saw a shift away from family-based care during the 20th century, particularly in industrialized nations.

The rise of urbanization, smaller nuclear families, and the increased participation of women in the workforce led to a growing reliance on institutional care facilities.

Nursing homes, assisted living communities, and other professional care settings became the norm for elderly care, especially as life expectancy increased and medical needs became more complex.

However, this model of elder care has come under scrutiny in recent years.

The high costs of institutional care, combined with concerns about the quality of care and the impersonal nature of these settings, have led many to reconsider the role of the family in caring for aging relatives.

Additionally, as healthcare advances have enabled more people to age in place—living in their own homes as they grow older—there has been a renewed interest in family caregiving.

Current Trends in Family Care

The trend toward family caregiving is growing, driven by several factors. One of the most significant is economic.

The cost of nursing home care in the United States, for example, can exceed $100,000 per year, a financial burden that many families cannot sustain.

Even with insurance or government assistance, the out-of-pocket expenses can be overwhelming. For many, caring for an elderly relative at home presents a more affordable alternative, especially when combined with home health services or part-time professional caregiving.

Cultural factors also play a crucial role. In many communities, there is a resurgence of traditional values that emphasize family responsibility and intergenerational support.

For instance, in Hispanic and Asian-American communities, it is common for multiple generations to live together, with younger family members taking on the role of caregivers for their elders.

This cultural expectation, combined with the desire to maintain close family ties, has contributed to the rise in family caregiving.

Additionally, there is a growing mistrust in institutional care settings.

Highly publicized cases of neglect and abuse in nursing homes, along with the isolation experienced by residents during the COVID-19 pandemic, have led many to question whether these facilities can provide the compassionate, individualized care that older adults need.

As a result, families are increasingly choosing to care for their elderly relatives at home, where they can ensure their well-being and maintain a sense of normalcy.

Case Studies

To better understand the shift toward family caregiving, it's helpful to look at some real-life examples. Consider the case of the Johnson family in rural Pennsylvania.

When their 85-year-old mother, who has Alzheimer's disease, could no longer live independently, the family faced a difficult decision: place her in a nursing home or bring her into one of their homes.

After weighing the costs and benefits, they decided to convert the basement of their eldest son's house into a living space for her. With the help of a home health aide and a rotating schedule among the siblings, they were able to provide 24/7 care.

The arrangement allowed their mother to remain in a familiar environment, surrounded by family, which significantly improved her quality of life.

In another case, the Patel family in California chose to care for their elderly father at home after he suffered a stroke. They made extensive modifications to their home to accommodate his wheelchair and installed a home monitoring system to keep track of his health.

With the support of a community-based caregiver cooperative, they received training in basic caregiving skills and were able to manage his daily needs.

This approach not only saved the family thousands of dollars in potential nursing home fees but also allowed them to maintain a close bond with their father during his final years.

These stories are not unique. Across the country, and indeed around the world, families are finding creative solutions to the challenges of elder care. Whether motivated by financial necessity, cultural values, or a desire to provide more personalized care, the trend toward family caregiving is likely to continue growing.

Section 2: Legal and Regulatory Framework

Legal Requirements for Family Caregivers

As the trend of family caregiving grows, navigating the legal landscape has become a crucial aspect of ensuring that elderly relatives receive the care they need.

The legal requirements for family caregivers can be complex and vary significantly across different regions and countries.

Understanding these requirements is essential to avoid legal pitfalls and to ensure that both the caregiver and the elderly person are protected under the law.

In many countries, caregiving by a family member is permitted and even encouraged, but it often requires adherence to specific legal procedures.

For instance, in the United States, family caregivers may need to obtain legal authority to make decisions on behalf of their elderly relatives. This could involve setting up a power of attorney, which grants the caregiver the right to make financial, medical, and legal decisions for the elder.

The process of obtaining a power of attorney typically involves drafting a legal document that specifies the extent of the caregiver's authority.

This document must be signed by the elderly person, provided they are mentally competent to do so, and may require notarization or approval from a court.

In cases where the elder is no longer capable of making decisions, the caregiver may need to petition a court to be appointed as a legal guardian or conservator, a process that can be lengthy and complicated.

Another critical legal consideration is the Health Insurance Portability and Accountability Act (HIPAA) in the United States, which protects the privacy of individuals' health information.

Family caregivers need to be aware of HIPAA regulations to ensure they have the necessary permissions to access and manage the elderly person's medical records. This often requires written consent from the elder or legal documentation proving the caregiver's authority.

In Europe, the legal framework for family caregiving can be different.

For example, in Germany, the Pflegezeitgesetz (Caregiver Leave Act) allows employees to take up to ten days of paid leave to care for a close relative in an emergency, and up to six months of unpaid leave.

However, caregivers must inform their employer and provide proof of the relative's need for care.

Similarly, in the United Kingdom, caregivers can apply for Carer's Allowance, a financial benefit, but they must meet specific criteria, such as providing at least 35 hours of care per week and earning below a certain threshold.

In other regions, such as Asia, the legal requirements for family caregiving may be less formalized but still present challenges.

For instance, in countries like Japan, where the aging population is particularly high, the government has implemented various support systems for family caregivers.

However, these systems often require caregivers to navigate a complex bureaucracy to access benefits and services.

Role of Health Providers in Granting Permissions

Healthcare providers play a vital role in the process of family caregiving, particularly when it comes to granting permissions and ensuring that the caregiving arrangement is suitable and safe.

Before a family member can take on the role of a primary caregiver, it is often necessary to obtain approval from healthcare professionals, who will assess the elder's medical needs and the caregiver's ability to meet them.

This assessment typically involves a thorough evaluation of the elderly person's physical and mental health, as well as their daily living needs.

Healthcare providers, such as doctors, nurses, and social workers, may conduct home visits to ensure that the living environment is safe and appropriate for the elder's care. They may also provide training to the caregiver on how to manage specific health conditions, administer medications, and handle emergencies.

In some cases, healthcare providers may recommend or require that certain home modifications be made before the elder can be cared for at home.

This could include installing ramps, grab bars, or medical equipment like hospital beds and oxygen tanks. Providers may also coordinate with home health agencies to arrange for additional support, such as physical therapy or nursing care, which can be critical for ensuring the elder's well-being.

Furthermore, healthcare providers are often responsible for creating a care plan that outlines the elder's medical and personal care needs.

This plan serves as a guideline for the family caregiver, helping them to provide consistent and effective care. The care plan may include instructions on managing chronic conditions, such as diabetes or heart disease, as well as recommendations for diet, exercise, and social activities.

In some jurisdictions, healthcare providers may be required to certify the elder's condition to qualify the caregiver for financial assistance or other benefits.

For example, in the United States, a doctor's certification is often needed to apply for Medicaid benefits or Veteran's Aid and Attendance, which can help cover the costs of home care. Similarly, in the UK, a medical assessment may be required to receive Carer's Allowance or other government support.

The collaboration between healthcare providers and family caregivers is essential for ensuring that the caregiving arrangement is successful and that the elder receives the appropriate level of care.

It also helps to establish clear communication channels, which are crucial for addressing any changes in the elder's condition or care needs.

Government Policies and Support Programs

Governments around the world have recognized the growing trend of family caregiving and have implemented various policies and support programs to assist caregivers.

These programs are designed to alleviate some of the financial, emotional, and physical burdens associated with caregiving, and to ensure that both caregivers and elderly individuals receive the support they need.

In the United States, one of the most significant support programs for family caregivers is the Family and Medical Leave Act (FMLA), which allows eligible employees to take up to 12 weeks of unpaid leave per year to care for a family member with a serious health condition.

During this time, their job is protected, and they can continue to receive health benefits. While FMLA is a crucial resource, it does not provide financial compensation, which can be a significant drawback for many caregivers.

To address the financial challenges of caregiving, some states in the U.S. have implemented programs that provide direct payments to family caregivers.

For example, California's In-Home Supportive Services (IHSS) program pays family members to care for an elderly relative who is eligible for Medicaid.

Similarly, the Cash and Counseling program available in states like Florida and New Jersey allows elderly individuals to receive a cash allowance that they can use to hire a family member as a caregiver.

In Europe, government support for family caregivers is often more comprehensive. For instance, in Sweden, family caregivers can receive financial compensation through the Attendance Allowance, which is part of the country's social insurance system.

Additionally, the Swedish government provides extensive support services, such as respite care, which allows caregivers to take a break while a professional caregiver temporarily takes over their duties.

In Germany, the Pflegeversicherung (long-term care insurance) system provides financial benefits to family caregivers, including a caregiving allowance and payments for home modifications.

Caregivers can also receive training and access to support groups through government-sponsored programs.

The German government recognizes the importance of supporting family caregivers as part of its broader social care policy, which emphasizes aging in place.

The United Kingdom offers a range of benefits for family caregivers, including Carer's Allowance, which provides a weekly payment to those who spend at least 35 hours a week caring for someone with a disability.

Additionally, the UK government offers a Carer's Credit, which helps caregivers build their state pension while taking time off work to care for a loved one. Local authorities in the UK also provide various support services, such as respite care, counseling, and training for caregivers.

In Asia, government support for family caregivers varies widely. In Japan, the government has introduced the Long-Term Care Insurance (LTCI) system, which provides benefits for both institutional and in-home care.

Under this system, elderly individuals are assessed by a local government official to determine their care needs, and family caregivers can receive financial assistance and access to support services based on the assessment.

In contrast, in countries like India, government support for family caregivers is limited, and much of the caregiving burden falls on the family without formal assistance.

Despite the differences in support programs across regions, one common thread is the recognition of the critical role that family caregivers play in the healthcare system.

Governments are increasingly aware of the need to provide financial, emotional, and practical support to these caregivers to ensure that they can continue to care for their elderly relatives effectively.

Section 3: Healthcare Implications and Challenges

Physical and Mental Health of Caregivers

Caring for an elderly relative can have profound implications for the physical and mental health of family caregivers.

While caregiving can be a rewarding experience, it often comes with significant challenges that can take a toll on the caregiver's well-being.

Physically, caregiving can be demanding, especially when the elderly person requires assistance with activities of daily living (ADLs) such as bathing, dressing, and mobility.

Caregivers may need to lift or move their relative, which can lead to back injuries, muscle strain, and other physical ailments. Additionally, the constant vigilance required to monitor the elder's health and respond to emergencies can lead to chronic fatigue and sleep disturbances.

Mentally, the responsibilities of caregiving can be overwhelming. Caregivers often experience high levels of stress, anxiety, and depression, particularly when they feel isolated or unsupported.

The emotional burden of caring for a loved one with a debilitating condition, such as dementia, can be particularly challenging.

Caregivers may struggle with feelings of guilt, grief, and frustration, especially when they perceive their efforts as inadequate or when the elder's condition worsens despite their best efforts.

Research has shown that caregivers are at an increased risk of developing mental health issues compared to non-caregivers.

A study published in the journal "Gerontologist" found that caregivers of individuals with dementia experience significantly higher levels of stress and depressive symptoms than caregivers of individuals with other chronic illnesses.

This stress can be exacerbated by the lack of respite and the constant demands of caregiving.

Moreover, the social isolation that often accompanies caregiving can contribute to mental health problems.

Caregivers may have limited time to engage in social activities, pursue hobbies, or maintain relationships with friends and family.

This isolation can lead to feelings of loneliness and exacerbate the emotional strain of caregiving.

The physical and mental health challenges faced by caregivers underscore the importance of providing them with adequate support.

Without proper assistance, caregivers may experience burnout, which can negatively impact their ability to care for their elderly relative and their own health.

__Training and Resources for Family Caregivers__

Given the complex nature of caregiving, access to training and resources is crucial for family caregivers.

Proper training can equip caregivers with the skills and knowledge they need to manage their relative's health needs, reduce the risk of injury, and prevent burnout.

Many organizations and healthcare providers offer training programs for family caregivers.

These programs cover a wide range of topics, including basic caregiving skills, managing chronic conditions, administering medications, and providing first aid.

For example, the American Red Cross offers a Family Caregiving program that provides comprehensive training on caregiving techniques, safety precautions, and emergency procedures.

In addition to formal training programs, there are numerous online resources available to family caregivers.

Websites such as the Family Caregiver Alliance and the Caregiver Action Network provide educational materials, webinars, and support forums where caregivers can connect with others who are in similar situations.

These resources can be invaluable for caregivers who need guidance on specific caregiving tasks or emotional support.

Support groups are another important resource for family caregivers.

These groups, which can be found in many communities and online, provide a space for caregivers to share their experiences, exchange advice, and receive emotional support from others who understand the challenges they face.

Participating in a support group can help alleviate feelings of isolation and provide caregivers with a sense of community.

Respite care is a critical resource for preventing caregiver burnout. Respite care provides temporary relief for caregivers by allowing them to take a break while a professional caregiver takes over their duties.

This service can be provided in the home, at an adult day care center, or in a residential facility. Respite care not only gives caregivers the opportunity to rest and recharge but also ensures that their elderly relative continues to receive the care they need.

Healthcare providers can also play a crucial role in supporting family caregivers by offering guidance, resources, and referrals to community services.

Regular check-ins with healthcare providers can help identify any emerging health issues in both the caregiver and the elderly relative, and ensure that the care plan is being followed effectively.

Healthcare System's Role

The healthcare system plays a central role in supporting family caregivers, particularly in coordinating care and providing necessary medical resources.

Effective communication and collaboration between healthcare providers and family caregivers are essential for ensuring that the elderly person receives comprehensive care.

One of the primary challenges for family caregivers is navigating the healthcare system, which can be complex and fragmented.

Caregivers often have to coordinate multiple aspects of their relative's care, including doctor appointments, medication management, therapy sessions, and hospital visits.

This can be overwhelming, especially when caregivers are unfamiliar with medical terminology or lack experience in managing healthcare needs.

Healthcare providers can support family caregivers by acting as a liaison between the family and the healthcare system.

This may involve helping caregivers schedule appointments, providing clear instructions on medication and treatment plans, and offering guidance on managing the elder's condition at home.

In some cases, healthcare providers may also assist caregivers in accessing financial resources, such as Medicare or Medicaid, that can help cover the cost of care.

Another critical aspect of the healthcare system's role is providing access to home health services. Home health services, which may include nursing care, physical therapy, and occupational therapy, are essential for many elderly individuals who are being cared for at home.

These services can relieve some of the caregiving burden by providing professional care and ensuring that the elder's medical needs are met.

Telehealth has also emerged as a valuable tool for family caregivers. Telehealth allows caregivers to consult with healthcare providers remotely, which can be especially beneficial for those who live in rural areas or have difficulty traveling to medical appointments.

Through telehealth, caregivers can receive medical advice, monitor their relative's health, and even participate in virtual support groups.

The convenience of telehealth can help reduce the stress associated with caregiving and improve the overall quality of care.

Despite the resources available, there are significant challenges in coordinating care between the healthcare system and family caregivers.

These challenges include communication barriers, limited access to resources, and the complexity of managing chronic conditions. To address these challenges, some healthcare systems have implemented integrated care models that bring together healthcare providers, social services, and community organizations to support family caregivers.

These models aim to provide a more seamless and coordinated approach to care, ensuring that caregivers receive the support they need to manage their relative's health effectively.

In summary, the healthcare system plays a vital role in supporting family caregivers by providing medical resources, coordinating care, and offering guidance.

However, there is still much work to be done to ensure that caregivers have access to the resources they need and that their contributions are recognized and valued by the healthcare system.

Section 4: The Business of Family Caregiving

Proliferation of Elder Care Companies

As the demand for family caregiving has surged, a growing number of companies have emerged to support families in their caregiving roles. These companies offer a wide range of services and products designed to ease the burden on caregivers and improve the quality of life for elderly individuals receiving care at home.

This sector, often referred to as the elder care or caregiving industry, has seen rapid growth in recent years, driven by the increasing number of aging individuals and the shift towards home-based care.

The increase in family caregiving companies that allow relatives to get paid for caring for their loved ones can be attributed to several factors:

1. Recognition of Informal Caregivers:

Many families provide informal care for their elderly or disabled relatives without compensation.

Governments and organizations are increasingly recognizing the value of this care and the burden it places on caregivers.

As a result, programs and companies have emerged that allow family members to be compensated for the care they provide.

2. Government and Insurance Programs:

Some government programs, such as Medicaid in the United States, offer options for family members to be paid as caregivers.

These programs are designed to keep elderly or disabled individuals in their homes rather than in more expensive institutional care. Caregiving companies often facilitate this process, helping families navigate the requirements and paperwork.

3. Growing Demand for Home-Based Care:

There is a strong preference for aging in place, where elderly individuals remain in their own homes instead of moving to nursing homes or assisted living facilities.

Companies that allow family members to be paid for caregiving help meet this demand by providing financial support to those who are already providing care.

4. Flexibility and Cost-Effectiveness:

Hiring family members as caregivers can be more cost-effective and flexible than hiring outside professionals.

Companies have developed business models that leverage this arrangement, allowing relatives to care for their loved ones while receiving compensation, often with lower overhead costs compared to traditional home care services.

5. Emotional and Personalized Care:

Family members often provide more personalized and emotionally supportive care than outside caregivers.

Companies that enable relatives to be paid for caregiving help ensure that care recipients receive the best possible support from those who know them best, while also relieving the financial stress on caregivers.

6. Economic Incentives:

For many families, caregiving responsibilities can lead to reduced income or even job loss.

Allowing relatives to be paid for caregiving provides an economic incentive for families to continue caring for their loved ones at home, making it a financially viable option.

These factors, combined with the growing recognition of the importance of supporting family caregivers, have led to the rise of companies that facilitate paying relatives for caregiving roles.

One of the most significant developments in the elder care industry is the proliferation of technology-based solutions.

These technologies, often referred to as "aging-in-place" technologies, are designed to help elderly individuals live independently in their homes for as long as possible, while providing caregivers with the tools they need to monitor and manage care effectively.

Examples of such technologies include telehealth platforms, remote monitoring devices, medication management systems, and wearable health trackers.

Telehealth platforms have become particularly important in the context of family caregiving.

These platforms allow caregivers to consult with healthcare providers remotely, access medical records, and receive guidance on managing chronic conditions.

Companies like Teladoc Health and Amwell have developed telehealth solutions that cater specifically to the needs of elderly individuals and their caregivers, offering services such as virtual doctor visits, remote monitoring of vital signs, and mental health support.

Remote monitoring devices, such as those offered by companies like Philips Lifeline and CarePredict, provide caregivers with real-time data on their elderly relative's health and safety.

These devices can monitor vital signs, detect falls, track daily activities, and send alerts to caregivers if any irregularities are detected.

By providing continuous monitoring, these technologies help caregivers stay informed about their relative's condition and respond quickly to any potential issues.

Medication management is another critical area where elder care companies are making a significant impact.

Companies like MedMinder and PillPack offer solutions that simplify the process of managing multiple medications. These companies provide services such as automated pill dispensers, medication reminders, and home delivery of prescriptions.

By ensuring that elderly individuals take their medications correctly and on time, these services help prevent health complications and reduce the burden on caregivers.

In addition to technology-based solutions, there has been a rise in companies offering in-home care services. These companies, such as Home Instead, Visiting Angels, and Comfort Keepers, provide professional caregivers who can assist with activities of daily living (ADLs), such as bathing, dressing, meal preparation, and companionship.

These services are often customizable, allowing families to choose the level of care that best meets their needs, whether it be a few hours of assistance per week or 24/7 care.

The growth of the elder care industry has also led to the development of caregiver support services. Companies like CareLinx and Care.com connect families with professional caregivers and provide tools for managing care, such as caregiver scheduling, payment processing, and care coordination.

These platforms often include features that allow family members to stay informed about the care being provided, even if they live far away from the elderly relative.

Another emerging trend in the elder care industry is the rise of care coordination platforms.

These platforms, such as Honor and ClearCare, offer comprehensive solutions that help families manage all aspects of caregiving, from coordinating in-home care services to managing medical appointments and keeping track of health records.

By centralizing caregiving tasks in one platform, these companies aim to streamline the caregiving process and reduce the stress on family caregivers.

Case Studies of Leading Companies

To illustrate the impact of these companies on family caregiving, let's examine a few leading players in the elder care industry:

1. Honor:
Honor is a home care company that combines technology with high-quality in-home care services. Founded in 2014, Honor has developed a platform that matches families with professional caregivers based on their specific needs.

The company's Care Team app allows family members to communicate with caregivers, monitor care, and receive updates in real-time.

Honor also offers support for caregivers, including training and resources, to ensure that they can provide the best possible care.

By focusing on both the needs of the elderly and the caregivers, Honor has positioned itself as a leader in the elder care market.

2. Home Instead:

Home Instead is one of the largest home care companies in the world, with over 1,200 franchises across multiple countries.

The company provides a wide range of in-home care services, including personal care, companionship, Alzheimer's and dementia care, and respite care.

Home Instead's approach is centered on providing personalized care that allows elderly individuals to age in place while maintaining their independence.

The company also offers extensive resources and support for family caregivers, including online training courses, support groups, and educational materials.

3. CareLinx:

CareLinx is an online platform that connects families with professional caregivers. Founded in 2011, the company has become a leading provider of caregiving services, with a network of over 300,000 caregivers across the United States.

CareLinx's platform allows families to find, hire, and manage caregivers, as well as track the care being provided through a mobile app.

The platform also includes features such as secure payment processing, care coordination tools, and access to a team of care advisors.

By leveraging technology to simplify the caregiving process, CareLinx has become a popular choice for families seeking in-home care.

4. Philips Lifeline:

Philips Lifeline is a pioneer in the remote monitoring and emergency response sector.

The company's medical alert systems, which include wearable devices and in-home monitoring solutions, are designed to provide peace of mind to both elderly individuals and their caregivers.

Philips Lifeline's products can detect falls, track daily activities, and connect users to emergency services with the push of a button.

The company also offers medication dispensing services that ensure elderly individuals take their medications as prescribed.

By providing continuous monitoring and emergency support, Philips Lifeline has become a trusted name in elder care.

5. ClearCare:

ClearCare offers a comprehensive home care software platform that helps agencies manage their operations and improve the quality of care provided to clients.

The platform includes tools for caregiver scheduling, client management, billing, and compliance tracking.

ClearCare also offers a family portal that allows family members to stay informed about the care being provided and communicate with caregivers.

By streamlining the administrative aspects of home care, ClearCare enables agencies to focus on delivering high-quality care to their clients.

These companies represent just a few examples of the many businesses that are transforming the elder care industry.

By leveraging technology and innovative business models, they are making it easier for families to provide care for their elderly relatives and improving the overall quality of care.

Market Growth and Future Trends

The elder care market has experienced significant growth in recent years, and this trend is expected to continue as the global population ages.

According to a report by Grand View Research, the global home care market was valued at over $340 billion in 2020 and is projected to grow at a compound annual growth rate (CAGR) of 7.9% from 2021 to 2028.

This growth is being driven by several factors, including the increasing prevalence of chronic diseases, the rising demand for aging-in-place solutions, and the growing awareness of the benefits of home-based care.

One of the key drivers of market growth is the increasing adoption of technology in elder care. As discussed earlier, aging-in-place technologies, such as telehealth, remote monitoring devices, and medication management systems, are becoming more widespread.

These technologies not only enhance the ability of elderly individuals to live independently but also provide caregivers with the tools they need to manage care more effectively.

As technology continues to advance, we can expect to see even more innovative solutions that address the unique challenges of elder care.

Another trend that is likely to shape the future of the elder care market is the growing focus on personalized care. As the elderly population becomes more diverse, there is a greater demand for care that is tailored to the specific needs and preferences of individuals. This includes personalized care plans, culturally sensitive care, and services that cater to specific health conditions, such as dementia or Parkinson's disease. Companies that can offer customized solutions are likely to have a competitive advantage in the market.

The COVID-19 pandemic has also had a significant impact on the elder care industry, accelerating the shift towards home-based care.

The pandemic exposed the vulnerabilities of institutional care settings, such as nursing homes, where outbreaks led to high mortality rates among residents.

As a result, many families have become more cautious about placing their elderly relatives in such facilities and are instead opting for home care.

This shift is expected to continue even after the pandemic, as families prioritize safety and personalized care.

Another future trend to watch is the increasing role of data and analytics in elder care. As more data is collected through remote monitoring devices, telehealth platforms, and care coordination tools, there is an opportunity to use this data to improve care outcomes. For example, data analytics can help identify patterns in health conditions, predict potential health issues, and optimize care plans.

Companies that can harness the power of data to enhance care will likely play a key role in the future of the elder care industry.

Finally, there is a growing recognition of the importance of supporting family caregivers. As the demand for family caregiving continues to rise, there is likely to be increased investment in services and products that support caregivers, such as training programs, respite care, and mental health resources.

Companies that focus on caregiver support are likely to see strong growth as families seek solutions that help them manage the challenges of caregiving.

In conclusion, the elder care market is poised for significant growth in the coming years, driven by the increasing demand for home-based care, the adoption of technology, and the need for personalized solutions.

Companies that can innovate and address the unique challenges of elder care will be well-positioned to succeed in this rapidly evolving market.

Section 5: Social and Cultural Impacts

Changing Family Dynamics

The shift towards family caregiving is having a profound impact on family dynamics.

As more families choose to care for their elderly relatives at home, traditional roles and responsibilities within the family are being redefined.

This shift is particularly significant in societies where the concept of extended family and multigenerational living has been in decline due to urbanization, economic pressures, and changing social norms.

One of the most notable changes in family dynamics is the redistribution of caregiving responsibilities. Historically, caregiving has often fallen to women, particularly daughters and daughters-in-law, who were expected to take on the role of caregiver for elderly parents.

While this expectation persists in many cultures, there is a growing recognition that caregiving should be a shared responsibility among all family members, regardless of gender.

In some families, this shift has led to more equitable distribution of caregiving tasks, with sons, husbands, and even grandchildren taking on more active roles in caring for elderly relatives. This can help alleviate some of the burden on women and create a more balanced approach to caregiving.

However, in other cases, the traditional expectation that women should be the primary caregivers persists, leading to increased stress and pressure on female family members.

The impact of caregiving on family relationships can be both positive and negative. On the positive side, caregiving can strengthen family bonds by providing opportunities for family members to spend time together and support one another.

Many caregivers report that they feel a sense of fulfillment and satisfaction from being able to care for a loved one, and that the experience brings them closer to the elderly relative.

However, caregiving can also create tension and conflict within families. The demands of caregiving can lead to stress, exhaustion, and feelings of resentment, particularly if the responsibility is not shared equally among family members.

However, in other cases, the traditional expectation that women should be the primary caregivers persists, leading to increased stress and pressure on female family members.

The impact of caregiving on family relationships can be both positive and negative. On the positive side, caregiving can strengthen family bonds by providing opportunities for family members to spend time together and support one another.

Many caregivers report that they feel a sense of fulfillment and satisfaction from being able to care for a loved one, and that the experience brings them closer to the elderly relative.

However, caregiving can also create tension and conflict within families. The demands of caregiving can lead to stress, exhaustion, and feelings of resentment, particularly if the responsibility is not shared equally among family members.

Disagreements over caregiving decisions, such as how much care is needed or whether to hire outside help, can also strain relationships.

In some cases, the emotional and financial pressures of caregiving can lead to rifts between siblings or other family members.

Another significant change in family dynamics is the impact on the caregiver's personal life.

Many caregivers, particularly those who are in the "sandwich generation," find themselves juggling multiple responsibilities, such as caring for children, managing a career, and providing care for elderly parents.

This can lead to a sense of being overwhelmed and can negatively affect the caregiver's mental and physical health.

In some cases, caregivers may have to make sacrifices in their personal lives, such as reducing work hours, giving up social activities, or postponing their own life goals.

This can lead to feelings of isolation and frustration, particularly if the caregiving role is long-term. It is important for caregivers to seek support and find ways to balance their caregiving responsibilities with their own needs to prevent burnout.

Cultural Differences in Family Caregiving

Cultural values and norms play a significant role in shaping how families approach caregiving.

In many cultures, caring for elderly relatives is seen as a moral and social obligation, deeply rooted in traditions of respect and filial piety. These cultural expectations can influence how caregiving is perceived, who takes on the role of caregiver, and how caregiving responsibilities are managed within the family.

In Asian cultures, for example, the concept of filial piety is a central value that emphasizes respect, obedience, and care for one's parents and elders.

In countries like China, Japan, and Korea, it is traditionally expected that children, particularly the eldest son, will take on the responsibility of caring for aging parents. This cultural expectation is reinforced by social norms and, in some cases, by government policies that support family caregiving.

In Latin American cultures, the importance of family and intergenerational support is also deeply ingrained.

Extended families often live close to one another, and it is common for multiple generations to share a household.

In these cultures, caregiving is typically seen as a collective responsibility, with family members working together to care for elderly relatives.

The strong emphasis on family ties and mutual support helps to create a sense of shared responsibility and reduces the burden on any one individual.

In contrast, in many Western cultures, where individualism and independence are highly valued, the responsibility for elder care has often been shifted to institutions such as nursing homes and assisted living facilities.

However, as discussed earlier, there is a growing trend towards family caregiving in these societies as well.

This shift is influenced by factors such as the high cost of institutional care, concerns about the quality of care, and a desire to maintain close family connections.

While cultural values can provide a strong foundation for family caregiving, they can also create challenges.

For example, in cultures where there is a strong expectation that children will care for their aging parents, caregivers may feel immense pressure to fulfill this role, even if they are not financially or emotionally equipped to do so. This can lead to feelings of guilt and stress, particularly if the caregiver is unable to meet the cultural expectations.

Moreover, cultural differences can also impact the availability and accessibility of formal support services. In some cultures, there may be a stigma associated with seeking outside help, as it may be seen as a failure to fulfill one's family duties.

This can prevent caregivers from accessing resources such as respite care, counseling, or professional caregiving services, which could alleviate some of the burden.

Societal Perceptions and Stigma

The societal perception of family caregiving varies widely depending on cultural, social, and economic factors. In some societies, caregiving is highly valued and respected, while in others, it may be viewed as a private matter or even a burden.

In cultures where caregiving is seen as a moral duty, family caregivers are often admired and respected for their dedication and sacrifice.

For example, in many Asian and Latin American societies, there is a strong cultural expectation that children will care for their aging parents, and those who fulfill this role are often seen as upholding important family values.

This positive perception can provide caregivers with a sense of purpose and pride in their role.

However, in other societies, caregiving may be viewed as less prestigious or even as a burden.

In some Western cultures, where independence and self-sufficiency are highly valued, there may be a stigma associated with relying on family for care.

Caregivers may feel that their role is undervalued or that their efforts go unrecognized by society. This lack of recognition can contribute to feelings of isolation and resentment, particularly if caregivers are expected to juggle their caregiving responsibilities with work and other obligations.

The societal perception of caregiving can also influence public policy and the availability of support services.

In societies where caregiving is highly valued, there may be more government programs and resources available to support caregivers.

For example, in Scandinavian countries, where there is a strong emphasis on social welfare, caregivers have access to a wide range of support services, including financial assistance, training, and respite care.

In contrast, in societies where caregiving is seen as a private matter, there may be fewer resources available, and caregivers may have to rely on their own resources and networks to manage their responsibilities.

This can create significant challenges for caregivers, particularly if they lack the financial means or social support to provide care effectively.

The stigma associated with caregiving can also have a negative impact on caregivers' mental health. Caregivers who feel that their role is not valued by society may experience feelings of shame or inadequacy, which can contribute to stress, depression, and burnout.

It is important for society to recognize and value the contributions of family caregivers and to provide them with the support they need to fulfill their role.

In conclusion, the shift towards family caregiving is having a significant impact on family dynamics, cultural norms, and societal perceptions.

As caregiving becomes an increasingly common experience for families around the world, it is essential to address the challenges and recognize the contributions of caregivers.

By providing support, reducing stigma, and promoting a more equitable distribution of caregiving responsibilities, society can help ensure that caregivers are able to fulfill their role while maintaining their own well-being.

Section 6: Ethical and Moral Considerations

Ethical Dilemmas in Family Caregiving

Family caregiving is fraught with ethical dilemmas that challenge caregivers to balance the needs and desires of the elderly with their own capabilities and limitations.

These dilemmas often arise from the conflicting responsibilities and emotions that caregivers face, such as the desire to provide the best possible care while also managing their own lives and well-being.

One common ethical dilemma in family caregiving involves the autonomy of the elderly individual.

As people age, they may experience a decline in physical and cognitive abilities, which can lead to situations where they are no longer able to make fully informed decisions about their care.

In such cases, caregivers may find themselves in the difficult position of having to make decisions on behalf of their elderly relative, sometimes against their wishes.

For example, an elderly person with dementia may refuse to take necessary medication or resist moving to a safer living environment, such as a family member's home or a long-term care facility.

The caregiver must then decide whether to respect the elder's autonomy or intervene in what they believe is the elder's best interest.

Another ethical issue arises when the quality of care is compromised due to the caregiver's limitations.

Many family caregivers are not trained healthcare professionals and may struggle to provide the level of care that an elderly person with complex medical needs requires.

This can lead to feelings of guilt and inadequacy, as caregivers may feel they are not doing enough to ensure their relative's well-being.

Moreover, the physical and emotional demands of caregiving can lead to burnout, which may further impact the quality of care provided.

Financial considerations also present ethical challenges. Caregiving can be expensive, particularly when it involves modifications to the home, purchasing medical equipment, or hiring additional help.

Families may struggle to afford these costs, leading to difficult decisions about how to allocate limited resources. In some cases, caregivers may feel pressured to reduce their own standard of living or sacrifice their financial security to care for an elderly relative.

This can create tension within the family, particularly if there are disagreements about how resources should be used or if one family member feels that they are bearing a disproportionate share of the financial burden.

The issue of privacy and dignity is another ethical concern in family caregiving.

As elderly individuals become more dependent on others for their daily needs, they may experience a loss of privacy and dignity, particularly when it comes to personal care tasks such as bathing and dressing.

Caregivers must navigate the delicate balance between providing necessary care and respecting the elder's dignity.

This can be especially challenging when the elderly person is resistant to care or when the caregiver feels uncomfortable performing certain tasks.

Moral Responsibility of Families

The moral responsibility of families to care for their elderly relatives is a topic that has been debated for centuries, with different cultures and philosophies offering varying perspectives on the issue.

In many cultures, the care of elderly family members is seen as a fundamental moral duty, rooted in values such as filial piety, respect for elders, and the importance of family bonds.

From a philosophical standpoint, the moral responsibility of families can be understood through the lens of ethical theories such as utilitarianism, deontology, and virtue ethics.

Utilitarianism, which focuses on the consequences of actions, would argue that the moral responsibility of caregiving lies in maximizing the well-being of the elderly individual and minimizing suffering.

From this perspective, families have a moral obligation to provide care that enhances the quality of life of their elderly relatives, even if it requires significant personal sacrifice.

Deontological ethics, on the other hand, emphasizes the importance of duties and moral rules. According to this view, the moral responsibility of caregiving is derived from a sense of duty to one's family, particularly to those who have cared for us in the past.

This duty is often seen as reciprocal—parents cared for their children when they were young, and in return, children have a duty to care for their parents in old age.

This perspective emphasizes the importance of fulfilling familial obligations, regardless of the personal cost.

Virtue ethics, which focuses on the character and moral virtues of the individual, would argue that caregiving is an expression of virtues such as compassion, kindness, and filial piety.

From this perspective, the moral responsibility of caregiving is not just about fulfilling a duty or achieving a particular outcome, but about embodying the virtues that are central to being a good family member. Caregiving is seen as an opportunity to cultivate these virtues and to strengthen family relationships.

However, while the moral responsibility to care for elderly relatives is widely recognized, it is also important to acknowledge the limitations and challenges that caregivers face.

Caregiving is a demanding role that can take a significant toll on the caregiver's physical, emotional, and financial well-being.

It is not always possible for caregivers to meet all the needs of their elderly relatives, and there may be situations where professional help or institutional care is necessary.

Moreover, the moral responsibility of caregiving should not fall solely on one individual within the family.

It is important for families to approach caregiving as a collective responsibility, where the burden is shared and everyone contributes in a way that reflects their abilities and circumstances.

This can help prevent burnout and ensure that the elderly person receives the care they need without overwhelming any one family member.

In conclusion, the ethical and moral considerations of family caregiving are complex and multifaceted.

Caregivers must navigate difficult decisions about autonomy, quality of care, financial resources, privacy, and dignity, all while balancing their own needs and responsibilities.

While the moral responsibility to care for elderly relatives is deeply ingrained in many cultures and ethical traditions, it is also important to recognize the challenges that caregivers face and to provide them with the support they need to fulfill their role effectively.

Conclusion

Throughout this book, we have explored the multifaceted aspects of the current trend of relatives being allowed and increasingly encouraged to care for older family members.

This shift towards family caregiving reflects broader societal changes, including the aging population, the rising cost of institutional care, and the desire for more personalized and compassionate care.

We have examined the legal, healthcare, business, social, cultural, ethical, and moral dimensions of family caregiving, highlighting the complexities and challenges that caregivers face in fulfilling their roles.

We began by discussing the demographic trends that have contributed to the growing need for elder care and the rising demand for family caregiving.

As populations age, the prevalence of chronic conditions and the need for long-term care have increased, placing significant pressure on healthcare systems and families alike.

This has led to a renewed interest in family caregiving, with many families choosing to care for their elderly relatives at home rather than relying on institutional care.

The shift towards family caregiving has been accompanied by a complex legal and regulatory framework that varies across regions and countries.

Family caregivers often need to navigate legal requirements related to power of attorney, guardianship, and access to medical information. Healthcare providers play a crucial role in assessing the suitability of caregiving arrangements, providing training and resources, and coordinating care.

Government policies and support programs, such as financial assistance and respite care, are also essential in helping caregivers manage the demands of caregiving.

We then explored the healthcare implications and challenges of family caregiving, including the physical and mental health impacts on caregivers. Caregiving can be physically demanding and emotionally taxing, leading to stress, burnout, and health problems.

Access to training, resources, and support services is critical in helping caregivers manage their responsibilities and maintain their well-being.

The business of family caregiving has seen significant growth, with companies offering a wide range of services and products to support caregivers and improve the quality of life for elderly individuals.

Technology-based solutions, such as telehealth, remote monitoring devices, and medication management systems, have become increasingly important in enabling caregivers to provide effective care.

In-home care services and care coordination platforms have also emerged as valuable resources for families navigating the complexities of caregiving.

Social and cultural impacts of family caregiving were also discussed, including the changing dynamics within families and the influence of cultural values on caregiving practices.

While caregiving can strengthen family bonds, it can also create tension and conflict, particularly when responsibilities are not shared equitably.

Cultural differences play a significant role in shaping how families approach caregiving, with varying expectations and norms influencing caregiving decisions.

Finally, we addressed the ethical and moral considerations of family caregiving, including the dilemmas caregivers face in balancing autonomy, quality of care, financial resources, privacy, and dignity.

The moral responsibility to care for elderly relatives is deeply rooted in many cultures and ethical traditions, but it is important to recognize the challenges that caregivers face and to provide them with the support they need to fulfill their role effectively.

Future Outlook

Looking ahead, the trend towards family caregiving is likely to continue growing as the global population ages and the demand for elder care increases.

Several key factors will shape the future of family caregiving, including advances in technology, changes in public policy, and evolving social norms.

Technology will play a crucial role in supporting family caregivers, providing them with tools and resources to manage care more effectively.

The continued development of telehealth, remote monitoring, and care coordination platforms will enable caregivers to provide high-quality care while reducing the burden on their own health and well-being. As technology becomes more integrated into the caregiving process, we can expect to see more personalized and data-driven approaches to elder care.

Public policy will also be critical in shaping the future of family caregiving. Governments will need to continue to recognize the importance of supporting family caregivers and to invest in programs that provide financial assistance, training, respite care, and mental health resources.

Policies that promote flexible work arrangements and protect caregivers' rights will be essential in helping caregivers balance their responsibilities with their personal and professional lives.

Social norms and cultural values will continue to influence how families approach caregiving. As societies become more diverse, there will be a greater need for culturally sensitive care that respects the values and traditions of different communities.

Families may also need to adapt to changing expectations about caregiving roles, with a greater emphasis on shared responsibility and the involvement of all family members in the caregiving process.

In conclusion, family caregiving is a complex and evolving aspect of elder care that reflects broader societal changes.

As the trend towards family caregiving continues to grow, it is essential to address the challenges and support the caregivers who play a vital role in caring for our aging population.

By providing the necessary resources, recognizing the contributions of caregivers, and promoting a more equitable distribution of caregiving responsibilities, we can ensure that elderly individuals receive the compassionate and personalized care they deserve while maintaining the well-being of their caregivers.

Please use the next few pages for your notes and debates.